D1709965

Where Did the Caterpillar Go?

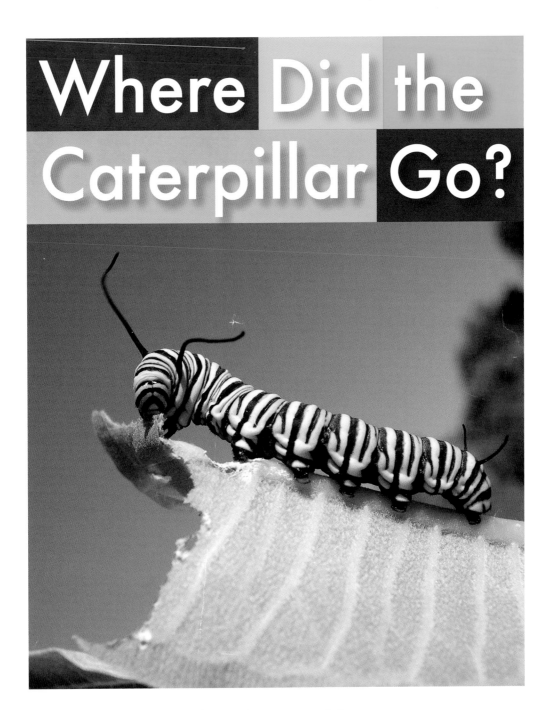

by Beth Bence Reinke

childsworld.com

Published by The Child's World®
1980 Lookout Drive • Mankato, MN 56003-1705
800-599-READ • www.childsworld.com

Acknowledgments
The Child's World®: Mary Swensen, Publishing Director
Red Line Editorial: Editorial direction and production
The Design Lab: Design

Photographs ©: iStockphoto, cover, 1, 7, 9, 11, 13, 17, 19, 21;
Shutterstock Images, 5; Christian Vinces/Shutterstock Images,
6; Steven Russell Smith Photos/Shutterstock Images, 15

ISBN 9781503807938
LCCN 2015958211

Printed in the United States of America
Mankato, MN
June, 2016
PA02299

ABOUT THE AUTHOR

Beth Bence Reinke is a registered dietitian with a bachelor's degree in biology education and a master's degree in nutrition. She enjoys writing children's books about science, food, nutrition, and race cars. Beth is also a columnist for her favorite sport, NASCAR.

TABLE of CONTENTS

CHAPTER 1

Where Did the Caterpillar Come From?

A butterfly flits from flower to flower. She sits on plants. She tastes each leaf. When she finds the right plant, she stops. The mother butterfly lays her eggs under a leaf. Then she flies away.

Each egg is the first step in the butterfly life cycle. A life cycle is a set of stages a creature goes through to become an adult. Inside the egg, the butterfly **larva** forms. The larva is called a caterpillar. This is the second step in the life cycle.

A mother butterfly may explore many plants
before finding the right place to lay her egg.

When it is ready, the egg hatches. The caterpillar bites a hole in the eggshell. It climbs out. Then it eats the eggshell.

Monarch butterflies lay many eggs at one time.

Tiny caterpillars hatch from their eggs.

The mother butterfly was smart. She laid her egg on a plant the larva likes to eat. It gobbles the leaves. Then it looks for more. It is always hungry. It eats and eats. The caterpillar may be tiny. But it has strong jaws. It can chew leaves all day.

As it eats, the caterpillar grows. Soon it is too big for its skin. A new skin forms underneath. The tight skin on top cannot stretch. So it splits open. The caterpillar wiggles out. Now the new skin shows. The caterpillar crawls from plant to plant. It munches on more leaves. It grows bigger. Then it sheds its skin again. It will shed its skin four or five times.

A caterpillar sheds its skin several times as it grows.

CHAPTER 2

How Does a Caterpillar Become a Butterfly?

When it is big enough, the caterpillar stops eating. It is time to become a **pupa**. This is the third stage of the life cycle. The caterpillar finds a safe place. It might pick a plant stem or a tree branch. The caterpillar spins a silk pad. The pad sticks to a leaf or twig. The caterpillar hangs upside down. Its skin sheds again. The new skin underneath hardens into a shell. The shell is called a **chrysalis**. The caterpillar hangs there, very still. It seems as if it is resting. But it is not. Its

The caterpillar's body starts to change inside the chrysalis.

body softens inside the chrysalis. Then it becomes liquid.

Soon new body parts form from the liquid. A head and eyes are made. Legs and wings appear. One day the butterfly is ready. The chrysalis cracks open. Slowly the butterfly pushes out. It hangs on the empty chrysalis with its legs. Blood pumps into its wings. The butterfly flaps its wings once. Then twice. Soon it flies away.

The life cycle of the new butterfly had four stages. They were egg, larva, pupa, and adult. First came the egg. Then it hatched as a larva, the caterpillar. Next, the caterpillar became a pupa. Inside the chrysalis, the pupa changed. It became an adult butterfly.

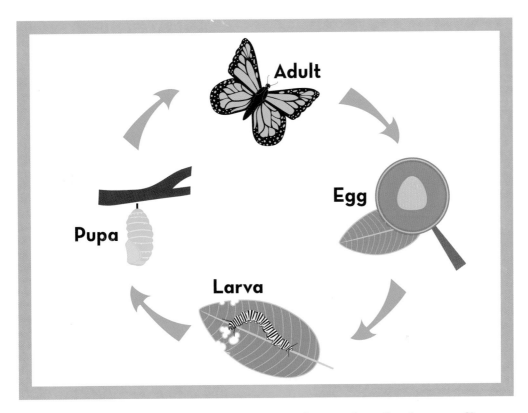

There are four stages in the life cycle of a butterfly.

CHAPTER 3

What Are Butterflies Like?

Most butterflies live for two or three weeks. Adult butterflies do not grow. They stay the same size their whole lives. Some butterflies are only as wide as a fingernail. Others are as big as a dinner plate.

Butterflies are a type of insect. All insects have six legs. Insects have three body parts: **abdomen**, **thorax**, and head. The butterfly's long tail end is its abdomen. The thorax is the middle. The legs and wings attach to the thorax.

Butterflies can be very brightly colored.

Butterfly wings are covered with tiny scales. The scales are brightly colored. They form pretty designs on the wings. Some colors and shapes on the wings keep butterflies safe. Dark circles can look like big eyes. Birds that want to eat the butterfly might be fooled by the circles. They might get scared away. And bright wings can be a warning. The flashy colors mean the butterfly tastes bad. It might even be poisonous. Birds see the colors and find a different snack.

Butterflies have two **antennae**, or feelers, on their heads. They also have two eyes. Butterflies drink a sweet liquid

A butterfly uses its long tongue to sip nectar from a flower.

they find inside flowers. The liquid is called nectar. Butterflies stick their long tongues into the flowers like a drinking straw. Sometimes they drink tree sap or juice from rotting fruit. When they are not using it, the tongue rolls up into a coil.

CHAPTER 4

How Are Moths and Butterflies Different?

Some caterpillars become moths. Moths and butterflies have the same four stages in their life cycles. The moth caterpillar hatches from an egg. Then it eats and grows. The caterpillar weaves a silk sack around itself. The sack is called a **cocoon**. Some moth cocoons hang under leaves. Others are buried in the dirt. The pupa changes inside the cocoon. It becomes an adult moth.

Both moths and butterflies are insects. But they have many differences.

Moth wings are usually brown or gray.

Butterflies are active in the daytime. Moths fly at night. Butterflies hold their wings straight up to rest. When moths rest, their wings are flat.

Butterflies have colorful wings. But many moths are brown and gray. The dull colors blend with night shadows.

Butterflies and moths have different body shapes, too. Butterflies have thin, smooth bodies. Moth bodies are wide and fuzzy.

Butterfly antennae are long and thin. Moth antennae are short. They look like tiny feathers.

Moths have wide, fuzzy bodies.

But both butterflies and moths start as caterpillars. The caterpillars do not really go away. They just change. Instead of crawling, they fly. Soon the moth or butterfly lays eggs. New caterpillars hatch. The life cycle goes on.

Butterfly Feeder

You can make a simple butterfly feeder using fruit from your refrigerator.

What You Need

A big plate
An orange
A paring knife
A cutting board

What to Do

1. Ask an adult to help you cut an orange into round slices.
2. Place the slices in a circle on a plate.
3. Set the plate outside in a sunny spot near flowers.
4. Watch for butterflies!
5. If you don't have an orange, other juicy fruits work, too. Try a slice of watermelon or grape halves.

Glossary

abdomen (AB-duh-mun) The abdomen is the rear end of a butterfly's body. The abdomen is one of three butterfly body sections.

antennae (an-TEN-ee) Antennae are feelers on an insect's head. Butterfly antennae are long.

chrysalis (KRIS-uh-lis) A chrysalis is a hard case that contains a butterfly pupa. The chrysalis hangs under the leaf.

cocoon (kuh-KOON) A cocoon is a covering of silk around a moth pupa. The cocoon is attached to a twig.

larva (LAR-vuh) A larva is an insect at the second stage of the life cycle. A larva looks like a worm.

pupa (PYOO-puh) A pupa is an insect at the third stage of the life cycle. A butterfly pupa is called a chrysalis, and a moth pupa is called a cocoon.

thorax (THOR-aks) The thorax is the middle section of an insect's body. Three pairs of legs are attached to the butterfly's thorax.

To Learn More

In the Library

Bishop, Nic. *Butterflies and Moths*. New York: Scholastic Nonfiction, 2009.

Marsh, Laura. *National Geographic Readers: Caterpillar to Butterfly*. Washington, DC: National Geographic Children's Books, 2012.

Merritt, Robin. *The Life Cycle of a Butterfly*. Mankato, MN: The Child's World, 2012.

On the Web

Visit our Web site for links about butterflies and moths:
childsworld.com/links

Note to Parents, Teachers, and Librarians: We routinely verify our Web links to make sure they are safe and active sites. So encourage your readers to check them out!

Index